UNSOLVED
AMELIA EARHART

DINAH WILLIAMS

Children's Press®

An imprint of Scholastic Inc.

Special thanks to our fact-checker M. L. Liu

Copyright © 2025 by Scholastic Inc.

All rights reserved. Published by Children's Press, an imprint of Scholastic Inc., *Publishers since 1920.* SCHOLASTIC, CHILDREN'S PRESS, and associated logos are trademarks and/or registered trademarks of Scholastic Inc.

The publisher does not have any control over and does not assume any responsibility for author or third-party websites or their content.

No part of this publication may be reproduced, stored in a retrieval system, or transmitted in any form or by any means, electronic, mechanical, photocopying, recording, or otherwise, or used to train any artificial intelligence technologies, without written permission of the publisher. For information regarding permission, write to Scholastic Inc., Attention: Permissions Department, 557 Broadway, New York, NY 10012.

The publisher and the author have made every effort to ensure that the information in this book was correct at press time. However, we recognize that new information is still forthcoming and that the nature of this subject matter in part lends itself to theories and first-person accounts that can be problematic to prove.

Library of Congress Cataloging-in-Publication Data available

ISBN 978-1-5461-4151-8 (library binding) | ISBN 978-1-5461-4152-5 (paperback)

10 9 8 7 6 5 4 3 2 1   25 26 27 28 29

Printed in China 62

First edition, 2025

Book design by Kay Petronio

Photos ©: back cover top: Everett/Shutterstock; cover main: Bettmann/Getty Images; cover airplane: Reuters; 1: Bettmann/Getty Images; 3 bottom: Reuters; 4: Scherl/Sueddeutsche Zeitung Photo/Alamy Images; 5, 6–7: AP Images; 8: National Air and Space Museum, Smithsonian Institution; 9: Science History Images/Alamy Images; 10: PA Images/Getty Images; 11: Bettmann/Getty Images; 12–13, 14: Scherl/Süddeutsche Zeitung Photo/Alamy Images; 15: Underwood Archives/UIG/Shutterstock; 16–17: Bettmann/Getty Images; 18: George Palmer Putnam Collection of Amelia Earhart Papers/Purdue University Libraries, Archives and Special Collections; 19 top: Reuters; 19 bottom: Jim McMahon/Mapman®; 20: Heritage Image Partnership Ltd/Alamy Images; 21: NY Daily News Archive/Getty Images; 22–23: San Diego Air & Space Museum Library & Archives; 24–25: Laurie Rubin for TIGHAR.ORG; 26–27: Joshua Stevens/NASA Earth Observatory; 28: Lightning Strike Pro/Adobe Stock; 29 all: TIGHAR.ORG; 30: Keystone-France/Gamma-Keystone/Getty Images; 31: George Palmer Putnam Collection of Amelia Earhart Papers/Purdue University Libraries, Archives and Special Collections; 33 all: TIGHAR.ORG; 34: Laurie Rubin for TIGHAR.ORG; 35: Charles Tasnad/AP Images; 36: TIGHAR.ORG; 37: Archive PL/Alamy Images; 38: Bettmann/Getty Images; 39: Frank Micelotta/National Geographic/PictureGroup/Shutterstock; 40–41: Deep Sea Vision/ZUMA Press Wire/Alamy Images; 42: SDASM Archives/Flickr; 43: Ben Margot/AP Images; 44 top left: Bettmann/Getty Images; 44 top right: Keystone-France/Gamma-Keystone/Getty Images; 44 center left: Topical Press Agency/Getty Images; 44 bottom left: PF-(sdasm2)/Alamy Images; 44 bottom right background: The Granger Collection; 45 top: David Buchan/Variety/Penske Media/Getty Images; 45 bottom left: Schlesinger Library, Radcliffe Institute, Harvard/Bridgeman Images; 45 bottom right: Deep Sea Vision/ZUMA Press Wire/Alamy Images; 46: The Granger Collection.

All other photos © Shutterstock.

INTRODUCTION: Disappeared! 4

CHAPTER 1: Amelia Takes Off 8

CHAPTER 2: Lost! 18

CHAPTER 3: What Happened? 24

CHAPTER 4: More Evidence 30

CHAPTER 5: What to Believe? 42

Timeline: Then and Now 44

Amelia Earhart's Fame 46

Glossary 47

Index 48

About the Author 48

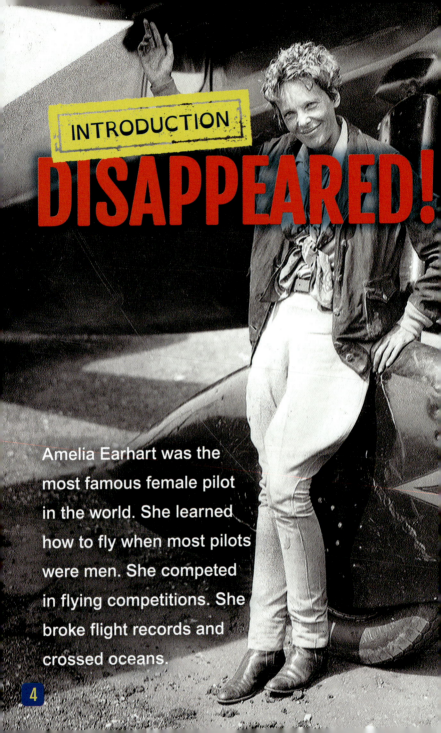

INTRODUCTION
DISAPPEARED!

Amelia Earhart was the most famous female pilot in the world. She learned how to fly when most pilots were men. She competed in flying competitions. She broke flight records and crossed oceans.

Then, Amelia came up with a big plan. She was going to be the first woman to fly around the globe! Her **navigator** was Fred Noonan. Their first attempt failed. On their second try, something mysterious happened. About a month into their trip, Amelia's plane disappeared.

Amelia and Fred disappeared in 1937.

The United States Navy looked for weeks. There was no trace of Amelia or Fred. They could not find their lost plane in the ocean. No one could figure out what happened.

Amelia and Fred review a flight map.

For many years, researchers kept looking for clues. What happened? There are different **theories**. And new evidence that could help solve the mystery. Let's explore what we know!

CHAPTER 1
AMELIA TAKES OFF

Amelia (left) in 1921 with Neta Snook.

Amelia Earhart was in her twenties when she took her first plane ride. "As soon as we left the ground," she said, "I knew I myself had to fly."

Not many women at that time were pilots. But that didn't stop Amelia. A female pilot named Anita "Neta" Snook taught Amelia how to fly. In 1921, Amelia had saved enough money to buy her own airplane. Amelia called the yellow plane *The Canary*.

The Canary was a single-engine biplane. It had two sets of wings.

Amelia holds flowers after her flight in 1928.

Amelia earned her pilot's license in 1923. At the time, only sixteen women had one. She flew every chance she had. In 1928, Amelia became the first woman to fly across the Atlantic Ocean. But she was a passenger, not the pilot. "I was just baggage, like a sack of potatoes," she said.

That would soon change. Amelia trained nonstop. She broke speed and **altitude** records. By 1932, she was ready to do it on her own.

FAMOUS FIRST

Charles Lindbergh was a famous pilot. He was the first person to fly solo nonstop across the Atlantic Ocean. He flew from New York to Paris in 1927. The flight took 33 hours and 30 minutes.

Lindbergh's plane was called the *Spirit of St. Louis*.

Amelia's plane took off from Newfoundland, Canada. She planned to land in Paris exactly five years after Charles Lindbergh. She flew east over the Atlantic Ocean. There were strong winds and icy storms.

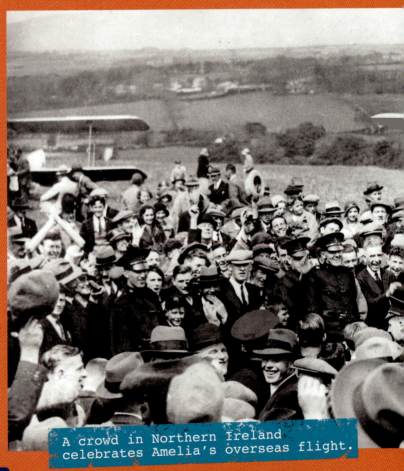

A crowd in Northern Ireland celebrates Amelia's overseas flight.

Amelia flew for about 15 hours. There was bad weather and problems with her plane. She was forced to land in Northern Ireland. But she had crossed the Atlantic nonstop on her own. Amelia was famous!

President Hoover (left) awards Amelia a gold medal in 1932.

Amelia broke another record in 1932. She became the first woman to fly solo across the United States and back. She was also the first person to fly solo from Hawaii to California.

These trips all led to her dream voyage. She wanted to fly around the world. Amelia made her first attempt in March 1937. She took off from California and flew to Hawaii. But she had trouble with her plane in Hawaii and had to give up.

Amelia checks her plane's supplies before flying to Hawaii in 1937.

15

Fred and Amelia in 1937. They are at a stop in Puerto Rico.

Amelia tried again that same year, on June 1. She knew the trip was dangerous. "I want to do it because I want to do it," she wrote. "Women must try to do things as men have tried."

She and Fred took off from Miami, Florida. They flew east nearly 22,000 miles (35,406 km). Along the way they stopped in South America, Africa, India, and Australia. They landed in New Guinea on June 29.

CHAPTER 2
LOST!

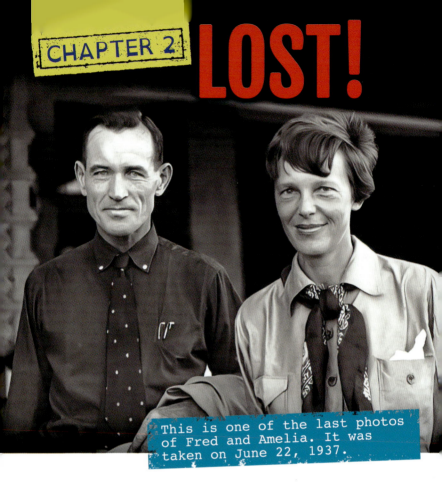

This is one of the last photos of Fred and Amelia. It was taken on June 22, 1937.

Amelia and Fred left New Guinea on July 2. Their next stop was Howland Island in the Pacific Ocean. Howland is only 1.5 miles (2.4 km) long. The weather was cloudy during the 2,556-mile (4,113-km) flight. They had trouble finding the tiny island.

They sent a message to a ship near the island. "We must be on you but cannot see you—but gas is running low." Did Amelia and Fred hear the ship's response? There is no record of it. That message was one of the last official contacts from them.

Amelia and Fred's World Flight Path

Amelia and Fred stopped in Lae, New Guinea.

Distress calls were heard in the days after they disappeared. Some of the calls were too weak to hear clearly. Multiple radio operators reported hearing a woman's voice. The voice said "water's high" and "send us help."

This is a Western Wireless receiver. Amelia was using a similar radio on her plane when she disappeared.

A New York newspaper headline from July 3, 1937.

Today we know more. Not all these calls were reported. Many were dismissed and not believed to be from Amelia.

The US Navy investigated the distress calls. They launched a huge search. It involved about 3,000 men, 102 planes, and 10 ships. But the search area of the ocean was the size of Texas. And the plane was sma

The Navy used planes like this to search for Amelia and Fred. It was called a Vought (vawt).

After sixteen days, the search was called off. The Navy made an announcement. The plane was lost somewhere in the Pacific Ocean. Or was it? Did Amelia and Fred survive?

CHAPTER 3
WHAT HAPPENED?

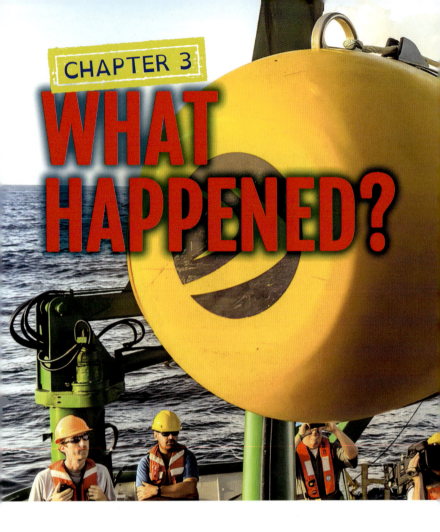

What could have happened that day? Maybe Amelia's plane ran out of gas. If so, it would have crashed into the Pacific Ocean. Both Amelia and Fred would have been killed. The plane would have sunk before the Navy arrived.

This is a type of deep-sea robot. It was used in 2012 to search for Amelia's plane. Nothing was found.

But the Navy never found Amelia's plane near Howland Island. Other groups have since searched the water many times. They used high-tech **sonar** and deep-sea robots.

There are more theories. Maybe the bad weather caused Amelia to fly too far. Maybe her plane ended up 350 miles (563 km) away from Howland.

Nikumaroro as seen from above. It lies in the Pacific Ocean. The island is about halfway between Australia and Hawaii.

The plane may have landed on the small island of Nikumaroro. No one lived on the island. It had no fresh water.

Nikumaroro Island is surrounded by a wide **reef**.

The Navy flew over Nikumaroro a week after Amelia and Fred disappeared. They circled the island again and again. But no one waved them down. So, they never landed to investigate.

A British officer took a photo of the island months later. His name was Eric Bevington. There was a shadow in the water. The photo wasn't analyzed until 2010. It could have been the landing gear of Amelia's plane.

Bevington's photo of Nikumaroro. The shadow on the left side is known as the "Bevington Object."

CHAPTER 4
MORE EVIDENCE

A British crew went to Nikumaroro three years later, in 1940. They were looking for a possible settlement. The crew discovered that someone had built a campfire on the island. They found a box. It once held a tool from a plane. They also found pieces of a woman's shoe. So, Amelia and Fred could have lived on the island for a while.

The British also found thirteen bones on the island. Scientists at the time thought they were from a man. The bones were then lost. They were never recovered.

Amelia and Fred at a stopover in India in June 1937. They disappeared about a month later.

Why didn't the British find Amelia's and Fred's bodies? There is one theory. Maybe they were eaten by giant coconut crabs. These island crabs can grow to be three feet wide. They have claws strong enough to crack coconuts. And scientists have confirmed they also eat meat.

Coconut crab

LOST AND FOUND

There are no images of the items that the British found in 1940. These items were found on Nikumaroro in 1991.

Amelia's supplies listed a knife like this one.

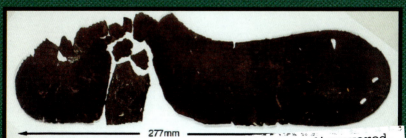

More pieces of a woman's shoe were discovered. They were put back together like a puzzle.

Richard Gillespie is a well-known researcher. His group has spent thirty-five years investigating. They want to know what happened to Amelia and Fred. Gillespie has written two books about their disappearance. He has a theory. Amelia and Fred landed on the reef at Nikumaroro. And the plane did not sink right away.

Richard Gillespie at Nikumaroro.

Gillespie discovered these items on Nikumaroro. The largest is a piece of an airplane panel. These might prove Amelia and Fred's plane landed there.

He believes Amelia and Fred sent distress calls from their plane. It took the Navy a week to fly to the remote island. By then, Amelia's plane was underwater. The pilots didn't see the plane from the air. So, they didn't stop.

There are more theories. Maybe Amelia and Fred landed safely on Nikumaroro. Then they were captured by the Japanese.

The Marshall Islands are northwest of Nikumaroro.

The figure circled on the left could be Fred. The figure sitting could be Amelia.

In 2017, a photograph from the 1930s was found. It shows a group of people on a dock in the Marshall Islands. Two of the people look like Fred and Amelia. The photo was later found to be from before 1937. The theory was proved wrong.

Amelia's height on her pilot's license was 5 feet 8 inches tall.

A new discovery was made in 2018. Scientists reviewed the notes about the bones found on Nikumaroro. They analyzed the bones' measurements. The bones were confirmed to be female. And the measurements were consistent with Amelia's.

Dr. Robert Ballard led a team to search the area around Nikumaroro in 2019. Ballard was famous for having found the wreck of the *Titanic*. He knew how to find things deep in the ocean. He spent two weeks and millions of dollars searching. But he didn't find Amelia's plane.

Ballard talking about his search for Amelia's plane in 2019.

39

Evidence found in 2024 points to a different story. An ocean exploration company used a robot to take deep-sea images. They discovered an object that could be Amelia's plane.

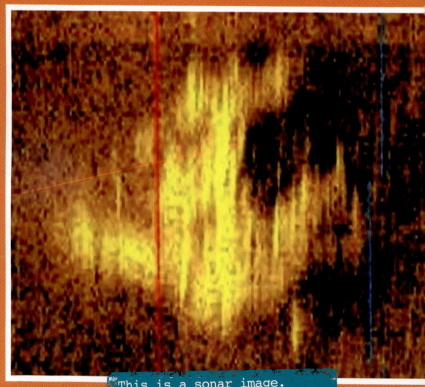

This is a sonar image. It could be Amelia's plane.

It was found 100 miles (161 km) away from Howland Island. It is so far down that they must go back to learn more. Could this be the missing plane?

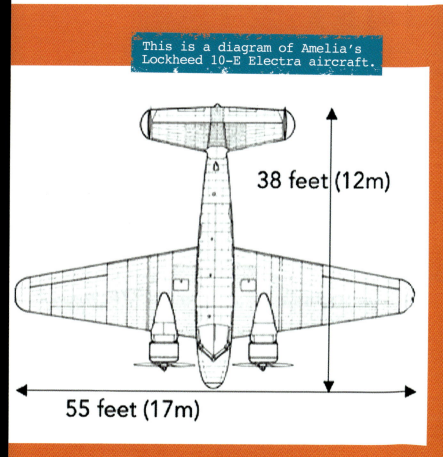

This is a diagram of Amelia's Lockheed 10-E Electra aircraft.

38 feet (12m)

55 feet (17m)

CHAPTER 5

WHAT TO BELIEVE?

So, what happened to Amelia and Fred? People are still trying to solve the mystery. It is important to ask questions. Why? Because not all theories are true. Some theories are not based on facts.

Without enough evidence, the mystery may remain unsolved. What do you believe? Maybe you're not sure. Maybe we can all agree on something. We hope this mystery will be solved one day!

A photo of Amelia from 1937 with a pair of her goggles.

TIMELINE: Then and Now

Amelia Earhart flies across the Atlantic.

British officials find evidence that someone was lost on Nikumaroro.

1928   **1937**   **1940**

JUNE 1: Amelia and Fred take off from Miami, Florida.

JUNE 29: They land in Lae, New Guinea.

JULY 2: Their plane disappears over the Pacific Ocean.

JULY 18: The US Navy ends the search party.

Dr. Robert Ballard spends two unsuccessful weeks looking for Amelia's plane.

2018 | **2019** | **2024**

Bone measurements from Nikumaroro are consistent with Amelia's.

Deep-sea photographs are taken of what could be Amelia's plane.

AMELIA EARHART'S FAME

Before her plane was lost, Amelia Earhart was known around the world. She was an inspiration and a role model for women. She was an **advocate** for female aviation. She had written two bestselling books. Amelia helped organize the first women pilots' organization. She received important awards and recognition. Three different presidents invited her as a guest to the White House.

Since her disappearance, she has been the subject of many movies. One of the most famous is *Night at the Museum: Battle of the Smithsonian*.

A US postage stamp honoring Amelia was issued in 1963.

GLOSSARY

advocate (AD-vuh-kit) a person who supports an idea or plan

altitude (AL-ti-tood) the height of something above the ground or above sea level

navigator (NAV-i-gay-tur) a person who finds where you are and where you need to go when you travel in a ship, an aircraft, or other vehicle

reef a strip of rock, sand, or coral close to the surface of the ocean or another body of water

sonar (SOH-nahr) an instrument used on ships and submarines that sends out underwater sound waves to determine the location of objects and the distance to the bottom

theory (THEER-ee) an idea or opinion based on some facts or evidence but not proved

INDEX

A
advocates, 46
altitude, 10
Atlantic Ocean, 10–13, 44

B
Ballard, Robert, 39, 45
Bevington, Eric, 28–29
bones, 31, 38, 45

C
crabs, 32

E
Earhart, Amelia
   fame of, 4, 13, 46
   first flights of, 9–10
   flights across Atlantic, 10, 12–13, 44
   flights across US, 14
   records broken by, 4, 10, 14
Earhart's world flight
   disappearance of, 5–6, 18–19, 44
   distress calls from, 20–22, 35
   evidence about, 28–41, 44–45
   first attempt at, 5, 14
   path of, 17–19
   searches for, 6, 22–25, 28, 39, 44–45
   theories about, 7, 24–29, 32–37, 42

G
Gillespie, Richard, 34–35

H
Hoover, Herbert, 14
Howland Island, 18, 25–26, 41

J
Japan, 36

L
Lindbergh, Charles, 11, 12

M
Marshall Islands, 36–37

N
navigators, 5
Navy, US, 6, 22–25, 28, 35, 44

New Guinea, 17–19, 44
Nikumaroro Island, 26–36, 38–39, 44–4
Noonan, Fred, 5. *See also* Earhart's worl flight

Pacific Ocean, 7, 18, 23–24, 26, 44
photo evidence, 28–29, 37, 40, 45

R
radar, 25
radios, 20
reefs, 28, 34
robots, 25, 40

S
shoe pieces, 30, 33, 34
Snook, Neta, 8, 9
sonar, 40

T
theories, 7, 24–29, 32–37, 42
transatlantic flights, 1

W
weather, 12–13, 18, 2

ABOUT THE AUTHOR

Dinah Williams, who loves all things spooky and mysterious, has written more than a dozen books for kids, including *Amazing Immortals*; *Terrible But True: Awful Events in American History*; *True Hauntings: Deadly Disasters*; and *Spooky Cemeteries*, which wor a 2009 Children's Choice Book of the Year Award.